Minnie,
you are my heart and my inspiration.
Always honor and embrace your rich heritage, mwanangu.
God bless you always.

Love,
Mommy

LANGUAGE KEY:
Mwanangu: my child in Shona
Rufaro: joy in Shona
Njabulo: joy in Ndebele
Thandi: love in Ndebele

Dear Readers,

Salibonani! Mhoroi! Hello!

My name is Rufaro Moyo. I am four years old. I am from Zimbabwe. I live with my parents and little brother, Njabulo, and my baby sister, Thandi.

My family speaks English, Shona, and Ndebele. I hope to teach you a few words in Shona and Ndebele by showing you my daily activities.

Come on, let's learn Shona and Ndebele! Huyai tidzidze ChiShona neChiNdebele! Buya sizofunda isiShona lesiNdebele!

Sincerely,

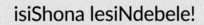
Rufaro

LANGUAGE KEY:
English Terms
Shona Terms
Ndebele Terms

www.mascotbooks.com

MY FIRST BOOK OF SHONA AND NDEBELE WORDS

Second printing. This Mascot Books edition printed in 2022.

For more information, please contact:
Mascot Books
620 Herndon Parkway, Suite 320
Herndon, VA 20170
info@mascotbooks.com

Library of Congress Control Number: 2020918104

CPSIA Code: PRT0122B
ISBN-13: 978-1-64543-811-3

Printed in the United States

MY FIRST BOOK OF
SHONA AND NDEBELE
WORDS

Written by Yeve C. Sibanda

Illustrated by Ariel Mendez

BODY
MUVIRI
UMZIMBA

Head
Musoro
Ikhanda

Hair
Vhudzi
Inwele

Face
Chiso
Ubuso

Neck
Mutsipa
Intamo

Hands
Maoko
Izandla

Fingers
Zvigunwe
Iminwe

Feet
Tsoka
Unyawo

Toes
Zvigunwe
Amazwane

Eyes
Maziso
Amehlo

Ears
Nzeve
Indlebe

Mouth
Muromo
Umlomo

Teeth
Mazino
Amazinyo

Legs
Makumbo
Imbala

Shoulders
Mapendekete
Amahlombe

Cheeks
Matama
Izihlathi

Stomach
Dumbu
Isisu

CLOTHES
ZVIPFEKO
IZIGQOKO

Dress
Hembe
Isigqoko

Jacket
Bhachi
Ibhatshi

Socks
Masvokisi
Amasokisi

Shirt
Sheti
Ihembe

Shoes
Bhutsu
Izicathulo

Trousers
Bhurugwa
Ibhulugwe

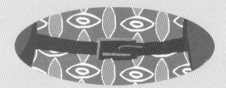

Belt
Bhande
Ibhanti

Glasses
Magirazi
Amangilazi

GREETINGS
KWAZISO
UKUBINGELELA

Good Morning
Mangwanani
Livukile

Good Afternoon
Masikati
Litshonile

Good Evening
Manheru
Litshonile

Thank You
Mazvita
Ngiyabonga

Yes
Hongu
Yebo

No
Aiwa
Hayi

How Are You?
Wakadii?
Linjani?

I Am Fine.
Ndiripo.
Ngiyaphila.

ACTIONS
ZVANDINOITA
ENGINKWENZAYO

 Laughing
Kuseka
Ukuhleka

Crying
Kuchema
Ukukhala

 Talking
Kutaura
Ukukhuluma

Standing
Kumira
Ukuma

Walking
Kufamba
Ukuhamba

Running
Kumhanya
Ukugijima

 Singing
Kuimba
Ukuhlabela

Clapping
Kuombera
Ukuqakeza

Jumping
Kusvetuka
Ukweqa

Sitting
Kugara
Ukuhlala

Reading
Kuverenga
Ukubala

TRANSPORTATION
ZVEKUFAMBISA
EZOKUHAMBISA

Bus
Bhazi
Ibhasi

Bicycle
Bhasikoro
Ibhayisikili

Car
Motokari
Imota

Motorcycle
Mudhudhudhu
Umdududu

Plane
Ndege
Indizamtshina

Boat
Chikepe
Isikepe

Train
Chitima
Isitimela

SCHOOL
CHIKORO
ISIKOLO

NUMBERS
NHAMBA
INOMBOLO

One
Potsi
Kunye

Two
Piri
Kubili

Three
Tatu
Kuthathu

Four
Ina
Kune

Five
Shanu
Kuhlanu

Six
Tanhatu
Kuyisithupa

Seven
Nomwe
Kuyisikhombisa

Eight
Sere
Kuyisitshiyanga
Lombili

Nine
Pfumbamwe
Kuyisitshiyanga
Lolunye

Ten
Gumi
Tshumi

Book
Bhuku
Ibhuku

Pencil
Penzura
Ipenseli

Book Bag
Bhegi
Isetsheli

Money
Mari
Imali

Teacher
Mudzidzisi
Umbalisi

Chair
Chigaro
Isihlalo

Desk
Tafura
Itafula

DAYS OF THE WEEK
MAZUVA EVHIKI
AMALANGA EVIKI

SUNDAY
SVONDO
ISONTO

MONDAY
MUVHURO
UMvulo

TUESDAY
CHIPIRI
OLwesibili

WEDNESDAY
CHITATU
OLwesithathu

THURSDAY
CHINA
OLwesine

FRIDAY
CHISHANU
OLwesihlanu

SATURDAY
MUGOVERA
UMgqibelo

MONTHS OF THE YEAR
MWEDZI WEGORE
INYANGA

January	Ndira	Zibandlela
February	Kukadzi	Nhlolanja
March	Kurume	Mbimbitho
April	Kubvumbi	Mabasa
May	Chivabvu	Nkwenkwezi
June	Chikumi	Nhlangula
July	Chikunguru	Ntulikazi
August	Nyamavhuvhu	Ncwabakazi
September	Gunyana	Mpandula
October	Gumiguru	Mfumfu
November	Mbudzi	Lwezi
December	Zvita	Mpalakazi

OUTDOORS
PANZE
PHANDLE

Moon
Mwedzi
Inyanga

Sun
Zuva
Ilanga

Sky
Denga
Isibhakabhaka

Cloud
Makore
Amayezi

Fly
Nhunzi
Impukane

Ant
Svosve
Ubunyonyo

Flower
Ruva
Iluba

Grass
Uswa
Utshani

Stone
Dombo
Ilitshe

Ball
Bhora
Ibhola

Leaf
Shizha
Ihlamvu

Tree
Muti
Isihlahla

Door
Musuwo
Umnyango

Window
Fafitera
Ifasitela

House
Imba
Indlu

ANIMALS
MHUKA
INYAMAZANA

Rabbit
Tsuro
Umvundla

Sheep
Hwai
Imvu

Frog
Datya
Ixoxo

Duck
Dhadha
Idada

Pig
Nguruve
Ingulube

Dog
Imbwa
Inja

Goat
Mbudzi
Imbuzi

Cow
Mombe
Inkomo

Horse
Bhiza
Ibhiza

Cat
Katsi
Umangoye

Chicken
Huku
Inkukhu

ANIMALS
MHUKA
INYAMAZANA

Monkey
Tsoko
Inkawu

Bird
Shiri
Inyoni

Lion
Shumba
Isilwane

Elephant
Nzou
Indlovu

Snake
Nyoka
Inyoka

Gate
Ghedhi
Isango

FAMILY
MHURI
IMULI

Father
Baba
Ubaba

Mother
Amai
Umama

Grandmother
Ambuya
Ugogo

Grandfather
Sekuru
Ubabamkhulu/Khulu

← Brother/Sister →
Hanzvadzi
Hanzvadzi/Mukoma/Muningina

Boy
Mukomana
Umfana

Girl
Musikana
Inkazana

Baby
Mwana
Umntwana

Mother's Older Sister
Maiguru
Umam'omdala

Mother's Brother
Sekuru
Umalume

Mother's Younger Sister
Mainini
Umam'omncane

Father's Sister
Tete
Udadewabo Kababa

Father's Older Brother
Babamukuru
Ubab'omdala

Father's Younger Brother
Babamunini
Ubab'omncane

MEALTIME
NGUVA YECHIKAFU
ISIKHATHI SOKUDLA

Cake
Keke
Ikhekhe

Vegetables
Muriwo
Umbhida

Bread
Chingwa
Isinkwa

Eggs
Mazai
Amaqanda

Potato
Mbatatisi
Igwili

Rice
Mupunga
Irayisi

Milk
Mukaka
Uchago

Bottle
Bhodhoro
Imbodlela

Pot
Poto
Imbiza

Knife
Banga
Ingqamu

Fork
Forogo
Ifologwe

Spoon
Chipunu
Isipunu

Chicken
Huku
Inkukhu

Meat
Nyama
Inyama

Cornmeal
Sadza
Isitshwala

Plate
Ndiro
Umganu

Cup
Komichi
Inkomitsho

Cold
Kutonhora
Umqando

Water
Mvura
Amanzi

Hot
Kupisa
Ukutshisa

Fire
Moto
Umlilo

ZAMBIA

•KARIBA

HARARE
★

•VICTORIA FALLS
•

ZIMBABWE

•BULAWAYO

BOTSWANA

SOUTH AFRICA

ACKNOWLEDGMENTS

This book would not have been possible without the support and encouragement of my husband, Arnold, and my mother, Liz. Shona and Ndebele are complex languages, and I would not have been able to accurately translate without the help of Julie, Max, Beauty, Mama, and Tuma.

I will be forever grateful to everyone who believed in this project and/or backed it financially. Ngiyabonga. Ndinotenda. Thank you. I would like to specifically thank the following individuals:

Mr. & Mrs. K. Perry

Ms. R. Chiposi

Mr. & Mrs. P. Chitiga

Mr. & Mrs. M. McFarlane

Ms. C. Akatugba

Ms. S. Sithole

Ms. B. Nyamolo

Ms. A. Seck

Mr. & Mrs. D. Madziwa

Mr. & Mrs. R. Mukushi

Ms. S. Ruzengwe

Mr. & Mrs. T. Chipunza

Ms. J. Rios

Mr. K. Hudson & Mr. L. Willoughby

Mr. & Mrs. R. Mukushi

Ms. L. Chitiga

Ms. P. Nyandoro

Mr. & Mrs. C. Okafor

Mr. & Mrs. W. Lindsay

Mr. & Mrs. T. Mutopo

Mr. & Mrs. M. Brooks

Ms. E. Aiken

Mr. P. Karoro

Ms. P. Takundwa

Mr. & Mrs. P. Mahefu

Mr. & Mrs. N. Daniel

Mr. & Mrs. A. Mbwembwe

Ms. C. King

Mr. A. Sibanda

Mr. Mrs. M. Mandigora

Mr. & Mrs. A. Toh

Ms. K. Masose

Ms. E. Ubiera

Mr. & Mrs. J. Osborne

Mr. F. Mugisha

Ms. C. Okeagu

Ms. A. Green

Ms. D. Robinson

Mr. & Mrs. A. Benedict

Ms. K. Hardy

Mr. S. Nguni

Mr. & Mrs. H. Mudawarima

A NOTE FROM THE AUTHOR

Shona and Ndebele are complex languages with various dialects spoken in different parts of the country. Therefore, there may be more than one Shona or Ndebele word to describe the same thing. I have attempted to use the standardized and widely accepted word in each instance.

ABOUT THE AUTHOR

Yeve is wife to her love, Arnold, and mom to her amazing and energetic daughter, Minnie. She is an author, attorney, and public speaker—and a creative at heart. Yeve prides herself on being a recovering Type A, designated sleep whisperer to her daughter (sometimes), intercontinental travel guru, and a quick-witted problem solver.

Yeve is a native Zimbabwean who calls the United States her adopted home. She wrote this book to help keep indigenous African languages such as Shona and Ndebele fun, alive, and interesting. She hopes to empower, educate, and inspire multicultural families to embrace their rich heritage and encourage their children to learn their languages.

www.philisacreatives.com

@philisacreatives

ABOUT THE ILLUSTRATOR

Ariel Mendez is an author/illustrator with a passion for children's literature. Ariel loves helping writers make their books a reality. She is a writing instructor and advocate for diversity in children's publishing. Ariel lives in Montgomery County, MD, with her husband, two sons, and dog.

www.arielmendez.com

@arielmwrites